A Beginner's Guide to Raising Sheep
Don't Be Dumb About Raising Sheep...Because They Aren't

By
Darla Noble and John Davidson

JD-Biz Publishing

All Rights Reserved

Disclaimer

Warning

Check out some of the other books

Entrepreneur Series books on Amazon

Science of Living Series on Amazon

Health Learning Series on Amazon

Gardening Series on Amazon

Table of Contents

Introduction

Most people consider sheep to be cute, wooly…and dumb. These same people would be wrong. The truth of the matter is sheep are cute and wooly, but as for being dumb…while it is true that some breeds of sheep are less resilient than others and don't do very well in the mothering department, the word 'trusting' is a much more appropriate adjective to describe these wonderful (yes, wonderful!) animals.

There are a few other adjectives which aptly describe sheep: manageable, functional and profitable. Whether you have a couple of acres or a couple of hundred acres—sheep have much to offer in the way of an agricultural venture *as long as you do it right.* That's where this book comes in.

"I cannot tell you how many times I've turned people away wanting to buy sheep; telling them to come see me when they are actually ready to buy." –Darla Noble

That's what this book is all about; getting you ready to raise sheep. Based upon the assumption that you've decided that's what you want to do, we will tell you:

*How to prepare yourself and your property to raise sheep

*What you need to raise sheep

*How to select sheep for your farm

*The primary functions of a shepherd (that's you!)

Chapter 1: Being Prepared... it's More than Just a Motto

So you've decided you want to raise sheep. That's great, but why? What brought you to this decision?

Is it because you think they're cute? Wrong reason.

Is it because you've decided both you and your land can manage and sustain a flock of sheep responsibly, with minimal difficulty and profitably. Ding, ding, ding! Right answer.

Grazing sheep

If you've answered correctly it is time to start getting your land and yourself ready for your livestock. To proceed before being ready is a recipe for disaster, or at the very least, disappointment.

I've seen it first-hand. People walk through the barns of a fair or farm expo looking at the sheep and talking to the sheep producers (farmers) about the benefits of raising them.

Sheep producer showing sheep @ farm expo

If they choose to ignore the farmer's advice on getting set up for sheep production (or talk to a farmer who is more interested in money than the industry itself), well, let's just say it's not pretty. They may come back to the same expo the following year, but their purpose is to tell off the farmer who 'lied' to them. It doesn't have to be this way, though, so why set yourself up for failure since you don't have to?

Think about it…would you turn your sixteen year-old loose with a car before he or she had any lessons on how to drive? Would you attempt to build something without any tools or the instructions or training to do so? I didn't think so.

What does it mean to be prepared?

To be prepared for raising sheep means you have what it takes to 'house', feed, water and care for them BEFORE you bring them home with you. Let's take a brief look at each one of these to explain why these things are important. The 'how' and 'what' of each aspect will be covered in its own chapter.

Housing for sheep is actually consists of nothing more than secure fencing and a place to get in out of the sun and cold wind. This 'something' can either be a barn, lean-to or even a line of mature trees on the south end of the property.

Fencing is *the* most important factor and the subject of another chapter. But for now let's cover the basics by saying this:

*Perimeter fencing for sheep serves two purposes: 1) keeping sheep in 2) keeping predators (other animals) out.

*Fencing should be used to break your pasture into different fields to enable you to implement a rotational grazing system.
Whether you have a barn, lean-to or merely depend upon a grove of trees for shade and shelter depends on a number of things:

*What you already have on your property in the way of outbuildings.

*How many sheep you plan on having, i.e. is it cost-effective for you to 'bother' building a shelter for a dozen or less animals?

*Where do you live and how harsh is the weather during the coldest and hottest parts of the year? The wettest?

Food & Water

The primary source of food for your sheep will be grass or hay. Supplemental minerals should also be made readily available 24/7. Corn and other grains will be fed at various times (more on that in chapter three).

Load of hay for winter forage

There are a number of livestock producers who claim that nothing more than grass or hay is needed to adequately sustain your animals. This is rarely true. Can they survive? Unless you are experiencing a severe drought, yes, they can survive. *But* surviving is not the same as thriving; thriving to the point of raising healthy lambs, being capable of breeding a number of ewes or growing a prime or choice carcass when processed.

In preparation for raising sheep you need to know how many animals your property can feed (supply grass for) under normal circumstances. This is called the 'stocking rate'. You also need to know:

*Where you will get the hay you need for the colder weather.

*Do you have a farm feed/supply store near-by from which you can purchase feed as well as other necessary supplies?

*Can you afford to purchase the hay and feed you will need?

*Have you learned (or are learning) how much to feed at different stages of the sheep's life?

<u>Water</u> is a must. If you have a pond or live-water source on your property you should take this into consideration when configuring the layout of your interior fencing (the fencing that breaks your property into smaller pastures or paddocks for grazing.

It's not likely you will be able to include a live-water source in every section of pasture so you need to make sure you can readily and easily fill water troughs with fresh, clean water from a hydrant.

*Can you supply the sheep with water no matter where they are at on your property?

*Is your water source viable during the harsh winter cold?

Sheep care & management

Last but definitely not least, let's talk about being prepared from a management and care point of view. If you have adequate fencing and shelter, a readily-available water source and pasture/food supply, you are well on your way to being prepared to care for your sheep. But there are a few other things you need to know. Well, actually there are LOTS of things you need to know but let's stick with the basics for now.

*Prepare yourself by equipping yourself with some general sheep knowledge in the following areas: breeding, lambing and the symptoms and treatments for the most common ailments and illnesses.

You can accomplish all of these things by networking with other sheep producers; preferably those who raise the same breed of sheep you are interested in. I know that might sound strange, but the needs and tendencies of sheep can vary greatly from one breed to the next.

Networking isn't the only way to learn, though. Farm expos, your county extension agent or farm service agent and websites devoted to sheep management and health.

Having the best fencing and shelter money can buy and all the food and water a sheep could possibly want is fine (but not necessary). But it's also completely worthless if you don't know what to do with the sheep residing there. You won't be able to prepare yourself for everything you need to know prior to getting your sheep because in all honesty, there are some things you just have to learn as you go. But by being educated on the basics, you significantly increase the degree of satisfaction and success in being a shepherd.

Ewe and newborn twins

By now you are either ready to keep reading so that you can get on with the business of raising sheep or have decided it's just not for you. I certainly hope you are eager to keep reading, because raising sheep IS rewarding, enjoyable and profitable when done correctly. So without further ado

Chapter 2: Fencing

As stated in chapter one, secure fencing is the first thing you need in place before you even consider putting sheep on your property. Woven-wire fencing or five strands of single-wire electric fencing is best for sheep.

Most people choose woven-wire for their perimeter fencing and either woven-wire or electric fencing to sub-divide their pasture for pasture rotation purposes.

Sheep in feedlot fenced with woven wire fencing

Don't make the mistake several have made; the mistake of thinking the old barbed wire around their place is suitable for sheep. Sheep can get out of traditional barbed wire fences; fences with three or four strands of wire placed 8 10 inches apart. These fences are meant to confine cattle. More importantly, barbed wire fences don't keep dogs or coyotes (a sheep's primary enemies) out. So if your place is fenced with barbed wire you need to either 1) tear it out and start fresh or 2) add one or two strand of electric wire between EACH strand of barbed wire.

Woven wire or electric wire—**the first thing you need to do is set your corner posts**. The corner posts are the perimeter markings of your fence. They should be heavy treated wood posts—four to six inches in diameter and eight foot tall so that they can be placed in the ground three feet deep. You can also use heavy metal posts if you like. They also need to be in the ground three feet deep but can be four to six inches in diameter.

Your corner posts are the foundation of your fence. The strength and stability of your fence as well as your gates hinges (pun intended) on your corner posts.

Electric fencing is not difficult to install. If you choose to use electric fencing, you will need to have access to an electrical outlet for plugging in your electric fence charger. This outlet will need to be in a barn or shed within the perimeter of your pastures because the main wires charging the fence will run from the charger to the fence.

To install electric fencing, you will need: high-tensil wire, a tool for cinching the wires TIGHTLY, metal posts and ceramic or plastic insulators (other than the charger and electrical source). The cost of materials is not unreasonable and the cost of electricity to keep the fence charged is <u>minimal.</u>

You will find that time and weather tends to loosen pull on your electric fence. The breaking of insulators also plays a major role in keeping your fence at its best. The insulators are inexpensive and easily replaced, however, so don't let this deter you from going the electrical fencing route if you feel this is what will work best for you.

Sheep and guard dog inside a high-tensil electric fence.
You have to look closely to see the wires in front of these sheep, but
you can bet *they* know the wires are there…and hot.

Warning: do not try to cut corners by buying cheaper and thinner
wire. You will NOT be pleased with the results.

Woven wire is a bit more expensive but is highly effective in keeping
animals where they are supposed to be. Woven wire requires a couple
of extra hands to install if you don't know what you are doing and,
like electric fencing, need to be cinched tightly. But when done right,
woven wire fences last for many, many years with little or no
adjustments necessary.

NOTE: Due to the roll of the land, many farmers add a single strand
of barbed wire at ground-level to their woven-wire fence to deter
curious lambs from getting out or predators from getting in.

Once you have your perimeter fencing in place, you need to work on
setting your interior cross-fences. These are the fences that will mark
your pasture off into smaller parcels called paddocks for rotational

grazing. When planning your interior fencing the two most common options are:

ONE: Woven wire fencing. Continuing to use woven wire will require you to anchor the ends of each cross-fence to the same kind of posts as your corner posts. While you may look at this as additional work, placing an additional anchor post or two (depending upon the size of your fence) actually serves to increase the strength and durability of your fence.

Using woven wire for interior cross-fencing is more permanent than electric fence wire and allows you to hang gates more easily. Gates? Yes, having a gate which allows access between each paddock is a *must*. Otherwise it will be impossible for you to implement rotational grazing…also a must.

TWO: Separating your pasture into paddocks using three electric wires is quick and easy. It isn't permanent, so you can change the size and location of your paddocks easily and it removes the need for interior gates—just un-hook the wires from one end and herd the sheep across to the next paddock.

If this is the route you choose to go you will also need to anchor the perimeter end of each cross-fence to a post like your corner posts. The reasoning is the same as it is if using woven wire. You can, however, hook the other end to eye hooks or a hook you make from wire on a regular metal t-post. You do this using an insulated 'gate'.

Deciding on which type of fencing to use is up to you. Deciding whether or not to do it right isn't—if you want to be successful, that is.

Chapter 3: The Three Essentials—Food, Water and Shelter

FOOD

Let's start with food. Feeding your sheep to achieve optimal breeding and lamb production in your ewes, ability to sire in your ram and carcass value in your lambs isn't rocket science, but it does require management on your part. Contrary to what some would have you believe, sheep (usually) cannot live on grass alone.

There are some places where this might be true—climates that enjoy year 'round grasses and legumes beneficial to sheep (ryegrass, timothy, brome, orchardgrass, kudzu, lespedeza, vetch and some clover and alfalfa).

Pasture of mixed cool-season grasses being mowed to scatter seed for re-growth before pasturing sheep.

But most of us experience cold weather or at least conditions in which frost kills the grass; reducing the nutritional value. This makes adding minerals and grains necessary for optimal health at different stages of their life. So in addition to grass and hay, your sheep need the following:

Minerals: A good *loose* mineral mix should be available to your sheep 24/7. The mineral should be a loose mix rather than a block to prevent them from breaking and wearing down their teeth prematurely. The mineral mix should include the following essential minerals and vitamins to a sheep's diet: sodium, chloride, calcium, phosphorus, magnesium, potassium, sulfur, selenium and vitamins A, D, E and K.

NOTE: do NOT use cattle minerals which contain copper. Copper is toxic to sheep.

Corn: A sheep's greatest nutritional need is energy; energy that comes from starches. Sheep need energy to grow, stay warm, stay cool, make lambs, make milk…live. (Don't we all?) Along with quality grass, corn is the best source of energy for sheep. Sheep need corn in addition to grass when they are in the final weeks of gestation into the first six weeks of raising their lambs for optimal milk production and during the extreme cold weather in order to stay warm.

Protein: The protein in a sheep's diet comes from legume hay and/or from soybean meal, cottonseed meal, alfalfa pellets or byproducts of distiller's grains. Depending upon the quality of your forage (grass), some producers feed protein to their ewes during the first few weeks they are producing milk to raise their lambs. Lambs need protein in order to grow and produce a meaty carcass of both monetary and nutritional value.

Lambs being fed grain and hay in late winter/early spring for the Easter market

How much should you feed your sheep and lambs? Read chapter five.

WATER

The subject of why water is essential is pretty much a no-brainer. Everyone and everything needs water in order to survive. So rather than talking about something you already know, let's talk about where and how to make water accessible to your sheep.
Aside from any live water you may have, you need to make sure there is a hydrant within easy reach (with a hose is okay). Some possibilities for achieving this are as follows:

*Place a hydrant or two on the outside of the barn (one at each end) and make all paddocks accessible to the barn. Then all you have to do is run a hose from the hydrant to the water tank you set within reach.

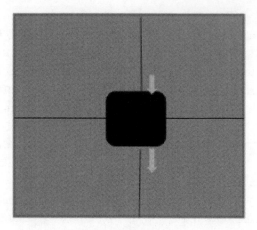

*Run a water line to the center of your pasture; taking in all paddocks. In doing so you will easily be able to reach each one with a short hose.

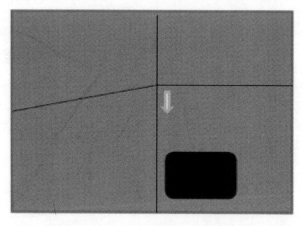

*Place a hydrant inside the barn and make it accessible to each paddock by using gates and multiple entries to the barn.

*For properties without an outbuilding, you will need to either install a hydrant at the junction of your cross-fencing or configure your cross-fencing to work with an existing hydrant.
Water tanks or troughs need to be:

*Low enough for sheep and lambs to easily drink from—no more than 10 to 12 inches deep. Anything taller presents a drowning risk to lambs. Don't laugh…I've seen it happen more than once.

---

*Kept clean. It is not uncommon for manure to fall into the water. When this happens the sheep will shy away from drinking the water (see, I told you they weren't dumb), which is a good thing because the fouled water is an invitation for disease-causing contaminants. The solution is an easy one: dump the water, rinse and re-fill.

*Set on a bed of 1-3 inch gravel or chat. The purposes in doing this are 1) to provide drainage so your sheep aren't creating a mud bath for their feet 2) the rock works as an emery board to keep hooves 'filed' down so you don't have to trim them as often if at all. The gravel bed doesn't have to be any deeper than 4-6 inches and should be faded out around the water tank 3-4 feet in diameter.

SHELTER

If you have a barn or lean-to on your property, you are a big step ahead of those who don't—but don't get too comfortable. You still have work to do to make your barn sheep-ready, but we'll get to that in a minute.
If you don't have any type of out-building on your property the first thing you need to do is decide if you need one. Does your property have a grove of trees that will provide sufficient shade and coverage from wind, cold rain and snow? If so, you should be able to get by without building a shelter.

Flock of sheep with a grove of trees as shelter

You will need to do a bit of extra planning when putting in your fence, though, to be able to work with and care for your sheep. You will need to construct a working facility/catch-pen in the center of your cross-fencing that can be accessed from every paddock OR build a working facility/catch-pen in one paddock and rotate sheep to that paddock when you know you are going to need to gather them up to wean, transport or work with them.

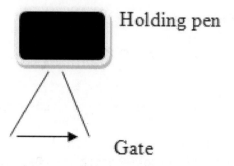

Holding pen

Gate

You will also need to make sure the pen is 1) truck and trailer accessible. This is necessary for transporting lambs you sell for slaughter, sheep you sell to other breeders or cull (remove) from your flock. 2) suitable for hold a ewe (or a few ewes) and their lambs if you find it necessary to seclude them for a day or two for lambing or health problems.

Truck and trailer used for hauling sheep and lambs

Okay, now let's get back to making an existing outbuilding sheep-ready or building an outbuilding suitable for sheep…

The purposes for having shelter for your sheep are:

Relief from the rain. Sheep don't mind being cold, but they don't like being wet…at all.

Relief from extreme heat. Who, or what, doesn't like a break from the sun?

Relief from extreme cold—especially cold accompanied by sleet and ice and wind.

A place to work your sheep, seclude mommas and their lambs if necessary and weaning, creep-feeding and sorting/loading sheep and lambs for transport.

If you have an existing building, you need to remove any built-up layers of straw, hay and manure and start with a 'clean' floor. In some cases there may be years and years of build-up. If this is the case, you will probably want to rent a bobcat or hire someone to clean the barn out for you.

Once you have the barn floor cleaned out, you need to make sure the gates will hold sheep (spacing between the ground and bottom of the gate and the gate's cross-bars). If not, don't worry about replacing the gates—just attach a 'wall' of chicken wire or woven wire to the gate.

Now it's time for the busy work—constructing a working facility/catch-pen and 1-6 lambing jugs (nursery pens). This is most easily and cost-effectively done by using hog panels. Hog panels are four foot tall heavy-gauge wire (metal) panels. Hog panels can be cut to size and even be used to make gates for lambing jugs. If you wire them together to be self-supporting, you can even fold them accordion-style against the wall when you aren't using them to make more room in the barn.

The number of jugs you build will depend upon how many sheep you have. If you have fewer than 20-30 sheep, a couple of jugs should do. If, however, you decide to increase the size of your flock, you will need to add more.

Newly-constructed barn with gravel floor

Lambing jug for momma and new babies

Other items you need to make sure you have in the barn:

*Moisture-proof cabinet to hold a lambing kit, halters, foot trimmers and other equipment

*Place to store hay that is not accessible to the sheep

*Truck-trailer accessibility for loading and transport of sheep

Prep time…food…water…shelter…*now* it's time to get down to the business of actually getting some sheep.

Larger lambing jug for momma and triplets to ensure all three are getting their fair share

Barn for sorting and holding sheep when necessary

Chapter 4: I Pick Ewe

Selecting sheep for your flock is something you need to put some serious thought into—particularly when it comes to the breed of sheep you choose.

What breed of sheep do you want? If you are new to raising livestock and want sheep that are hardy, productive and provide tasty and nutritional meat, you should choose the Katahdin.

Selecting sheep for your flock is something you need to put some serious thought into—particularly when it comes to the breed of sheep you choose.

What breed of sheep do you want? If you are new to raising livestock and want sheep that are hardy, productive and provide tasty and nutritional meat, you should choose the Katahdin.

Are you a craftsman interested in having your own wool to dye and spin? The Karakul, Angora, Romney or Merino will best suit.

To grow large lambs quickly, the Columbia, Tunas, Corriedale, Hampshire or Lincolns are hardy enough and easy to work with.

Do you want something to eat grass, look cute and possibly serve as a draw for farm tours? Babydoll sheep come by their name honestly.

Hampshire lamb being prepared for 4-H show

When choosing which breed of sheep you want to raise don't base your decision solely on what you read. Talk to people who raise the breed of sheep you are interested in. Take in a few county fairs, you state's fair and other farm and agriculture shows to compare different breeds for yourself.

Talk with people who are neutral on the subject matter; a county extension agent, vo-ag teacher or someone in the animal science school at a local university.

Once you are set on the breed of sheep you are going to buy, you need to make sure you buy healthy, hardy stock from a reputable breeder. This means:

*Never purchasing animals from a sale barn or livestock auction. Even if the sheep are healthy when they arrive, the chances of contracting illnesses and diseases is HIGH. Sale barns are for market animals (those going to the processor for meat).

*Try to buy all your ewes from one breeder and your ram from another breed.

*Start small. You can always buy more or retain your ewe lambs if you have the grass and room to accommodate more sheep.

*Visit the farm you buy from. Look at all the animals they have— even those that aren't for sale. Do they look healthy? Are they being managed well? Is their confirmation (body structure) everything it should be? It's also okay to ask for references and talk to other people who have purchased sheep from the same farm.

At this point you are probably thinking "I don't know. What does a healthy sheep look like? How do I know if their confirmation is right?" These are great questions and questions you should be asking, so let's take a few minutes to answer them...

Healthy sheep:

> Have bright, clear eyes
> Have a clean rear free of wet or dry manure caked to it
>
> Don't limp
>
> Aren't wheezing or have labored breathing
>
> Don't look too thin or too fat

NOTE: Ewes at the end of feeding lambs will often look a bit drawn, but that is to be expected.

Healthy ewe with excellent confirmation

You also need to take a close look around the farm. Do any of the other animals exhibit poor health? Are there foul smells (no, not manure)? Is their water clean?

A solid confirmation:

Short, smooth transition between neck and body and from chest to sides

Even, straight line (with minimal curving) in the hind legs when looking at the sheep from the back

Straight top line from shoulders to rear

Smooth, rounded rump (rear-end)

Four legs that sit squarely on each 'corner' of the body rather than being inset

Your ram should be thick, muscular and a twin. NOTE: One ram can easily breed up to 50 ewes.

Strong, muscular

Other things to look for:

Black hooves tend to be harder and require less trimming.

Hair sheep should have a coat that resembles a dog's coat (except in the early spring when they shed or mid-late winter when they sometimes carry a bit of wool).

If buying registered stock you need to receive the paperwork to transfer ownership and registration.

Pricing will vary from producer to producer, but it shouldn't vary by too much. Compare prices and don't be afraid to bargain (just don't be insulting). You also need to expect to pay more for a ram than you will for ewes.

Chapter 5: Hello, my Name is Shepherd

We've covered a lot of ground (literally and figuratively speaking) so far when it comes to what you need in order to raise sheep successfully. And while it all involves you; manual labor and learning/research, we've yet to discuss the day to day work involved with being a shepherd…until now, that is.

What follows is a simple list of chores a shepherd does on a daily, weekly or monthly basis. We won't go into great detail but will give you the basics of why and how you need to do each of them.

Daily feeding and watering: Make sure the sheep have clean water and that they have plenty of grass or hay to eat. If feeding corn or other grains to lactating ewes and growing lambs, do so consistently and at the following rates:

One pound of shell corn (not cracked) per lactating ewe TWICE a day

A handful of protein-rich lamb pellets per lamb starting at day 10, increasing to two percent of the average lamb's weight per lamb at one month and increasing weekly thereafter to maintain a two percent ration.

Example: If the average weight of your lambs at one month of age is 16 pounds and you have 10 lambs, you will feed a total of 3 (rounding down 3.2) pounds of feed to the lambs once a day. Each week increase the amount of feed accordingly and increase the feeding to twice a week at two months.

Rotational grazing: Rotate sheep through each paddock when they have eaten the grass down to a height of 2-3 inches. If at all possible, don't allow sheep back onto a paddock within a thirty day period to help control parasites. NOTE: Because this is not always possible it may be best to rotate them through the cycle every few days instead of basing it on grass height to help control parasites.

Be vigilant: An ounce of prevention is worth pounds of cure when it comes to sheep. Being aware of the earliest signs of parasite infestation (worms) or other sickness/disease can save you a lot of work and the life of your sheep. Watch for dirty butts, irregular breathing, lameness, lethargy, bloating (extended stomachs) and refusal to eat. Treat accordingly.

Don't overmedicate: If you manage your sheep well, the chances are excellent that you will never have to worm an adult ewe. Co-author, Darla Noble, raised sheep for over twenty years with a flock of 400 to 500 ewes (plus lambs). Other than worming the ewe lambs being kept for the flock or sold as breeding stock when they were weaned (two treatments 28 days apart), she never wormed any of the flock unless they showed signs of need it—which was rare. Worming medications are like antibiotics—overuse renders them ineffective. Remember that.

Breed responsibly: It won't matter if your lambs are excellent quality lambs if they aren't at the desired selling weight at peak market times, you won't get the price you should and could for them. In order to get the most for your lambs you need to have them ready for the Easter market and for Islamic holiday markets. So what does this mean? It means your lambs need to be sold two to three weeks prior to the actual holiday so they will have time to make it from processor to grocery store shelves. It is equally important to have lambs at the desired weights for these holidays. Traditionally lambs sold for Easter sell best when they weigh between 45-55 pounds. For Islamic holidays, the desired weights usually run between 70-80 pounds. This means you need to breed your sheep to lamb (5 month's gestation) in time for you to feed them out to the desired weights for these prime holiday markets.

Network: The people you talked to at the farm show way back when you first thought about raising sheep are there to promote the industry of agriculture, their particular breed of sheep and their own individual farm sales. You need to be willing to do the same.

Guard animals: Most shepherds like to have a guard animal with their sheep. The most popular choice is a guard dog; Great Pyrenees, Maremma or Sheep dog. The downside to using a dog is the fact that most people tend to make the dog a pet rather than treating it as a working animal. You also have to feed the dog differently. Llamas and donkeys make good guards and can be fed the same thing as the sheep. You will need to decide what works best for you. If you don't have many sheep and have the ability to shut them in a barn lot at night, this can also serve as a means of protection against predators.

Keep learning: As stated in the first few pages of this book, there is no way you can go into raising sheep knowing everything you need to know. Keep learning through networking with other producers, reading/research and by attending seminars.

Llama used to guard sheep

Conclusion

This book is only the tip of the proverbial iceberg when it comes to raising sheep. Don't worry, though, because this is only the first in a series of three books to guide you toward shepherding a healthy, happy, profitable flock of sheep. If, however, you find you cannot wait or have questions you need answers to now, contact Darla Noble at darlajnoble@yahoo.com and put the words 'sheep question' in the subject line.

Author Bio

Darla Noble is a native of mid-Missouri with over twenty-five years of experience as an author and ghostwriter. Darla's love of writing began in the fourth grade; after meeting up and coming children's author, Judy Blume, who, by the way, autographed Darla's copy of "Are you there, God...it's me, Margaret".

Darla's love for writing and family makes her work sought after in the Christian market, in the areas of parenting/family resources and inspirational nonfiction as well as working as a ghostwriter for educators and inspirational speakers. For more information about Darla as well as her other books, you can visit her website: www.dnoblewrites.webstarts.com.

Health Learning Series

Amazing Animal Book Series

Learn To Draw Series

How to Build and Plan Books

Entrepreneur Book Series

This book is published by

JD-Biz Corp

P O Box 374

Mendon, Utah 84325

http://www.jd-biz.com/

Read more books from

Mendon Cottage Books

P O Box 374, Mendon Utah 84325

Printed in Great Britain
by Amazon